★ IT'S MY STATE! ★

Alaska

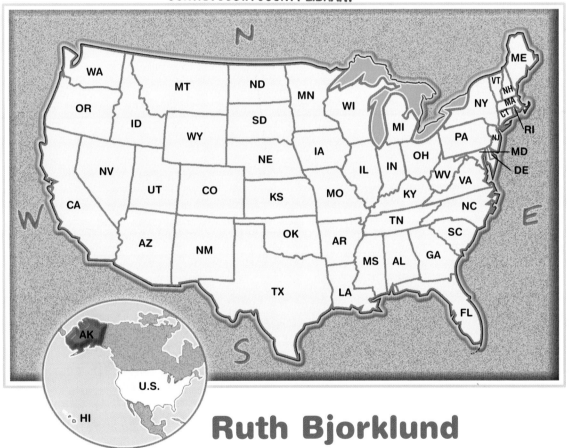

Ruth Bjorklund

BENCHMARK BOOKS

MARSHALL CAVENDISH
NEW YORK

For Neil, who loves snow

Benchmark Books
Marshall Cavendish
99 White Plains Road
Tarrytown, New York 10591-9001
www.marshallcavendish.com

Text, maps, and illustrations copyright © 2005 by Marshall Cavendish Corporation

Map and Illustrations by Christopher Santoro

Library of Congress Cataloging-in-Publication Data
Bjorklund, Ruth.
Alaska / by Ruth Bjorklund.
p. cm. — (It's my state!)
Includes bibliographical references and index.
ISBN 0-7614-1823-7
1. Alaska--Juvenile literature. I. Title. II. Series.

F904.3.B56 2004
979.8—dc22
2004010635

Photo research by Candlepants Incorporated

Cover photograph: Paul Souders/Accent Alaska

Back cover illustration: The license plate shows Alaska's postal abbreviation, followed by its year of statehood.

The photographs in this book are used by permission and through the courtesy of: *Accent Alaska:* Ray Hafen, 4 (top), 20 (bottom), 64; Loren Taft, 5 (bottom); Kim Heacox, 8; Ken Graham, 11, 48, 67, 68 (bottom); Tom Walker, 15, 69 (top); Caroline Fogg, 17; Cary Anderson, 18; Dicon Joseph, 19, 51; Stacy Schulz, 23; Luciana Whitaker, 40; Bill Bacon, 42; Dan Evans, 44; Paul Souders, 54, 71; Mark Yezbick, 55; Jim Rosen, 46 (left); Josh Roper, 65; Steve Gibson, 72; Steve Bly, 69 (bottom). *Corbis:* 37, 39 (top), 46 (middle); Darrell Gulin, 4 (middle), 14; Tom Bean, 9; Galen Rowell, 13, 53; Kennan Ward, 20 (top); Robert Holmes, 20 (middle); Steve Kaufman, 20 (bottom); D. Robert & Lorri Franz, 20 (top); Hal Horwitz, 20 (middle); Museum of History and Industry, 24; Bettmann, 36; Gary Braasch, 38; Roy Corral, 39 (bottom); Bob Rowan Progressive Image, 45; Underwood & Underwood, 46 (top); Mitchell Gerber, 46 (middle); The Mariner's Museum, 47 (bottom); Natalie Fobes, 70; Peter Beck, 74; Tim Thompson, 68 (top); Tom Bean, 68 (middle); Peter Guttman, 69 (middle). *Minden:* Michio Hoshino, 5 (top); Flip Nicklin, 5 (middle). *Photo Researcher:* Thomas & Pat Leeson, 4 (bottom). *Art Resource, NY:* Werner Forman, 27; Snark, 34. *Index Stock Imagery:* Omni Photo Communications Inc., 28; Yvette Cardozo, 43. *North Wind Picture Archive:* 29, 31. *Alaska State Library Photo:* Ward Wells / Ward Wells Collection #013294, 46 (top). *Robertstock:* R. Krubner, 56; R. Gilbert, 62.

Book design by Anahid Hamparian

Printed in Italy

1   3   5   6   4   2

Contents

A Quick Look at Alaska

Nickname: The Last Frontier
Population: 634,892 (2001 estimate)
Statehood: January 3, 1959

Flower: Forget-Me-Not

In June and July, forget-me-nots bloom on the tundra and throughout all of Alaska near streams and wetlands. The light blue flowers have five petals and a yellow center. When the flower was officially adopted, an Alaskan poet wrote, "So although they say we're living / In the land that God forgot, We'll recall Alaska to them / With our blue Forget-me-not."

Bird: Willow Ptarmigan

The willow ptarmigan is a relative of the arctic grouse and lives in Alaska's tundra and high alpine areas. In the winter, these birds have white feathers to help them hide in the snow. In the summer and fall, however, they have brown feathers to help them blend in with the ground and plants.

Fish: King Salmon

King salmon are the largest of all Pacific salmon. They generally weigh 30 pounds or more. Other names for the king salmon are Chinook, tyee, and blackmouth. King salmon have always been important to the diet of Alaskans.

4

Land Mammal: Moose

The moose is the largest member of the deer family and can stand as tall as 7 1/2 feet. Its large, partly flat antlers can sometimes be as wide as 5 to 6 feet. One moose can eat more than 40 pounds of twigs, bark, needles, tree roots, water plants, and willow and birch leaves each day.

Marine Mammal: Bowhead Whale

Bowhead whales are large baleen whales. Baleen is a fingernail-like substance that is found in this whale's mouth. The whales use baleen to filter the food from the water. Bowheads grow to sixty feet and weigh sixty tons. They never leave the Arctic, and swim under the winter ice and use their heads to smash up through the ice to blow. The whales are prized for their blubber (fat). Eskimos hunted bowheads in small, walrus-hide boats called umiaks.

Tree: Sitka Spruce

In the rainforests of southeastern Alaska, Sitka spruce can grow to heights of 200 feet or more. Native Americans have always used the tree to make ceremonial art, such as totems, masks, charms, and other carvings. Today the trees are used for house construction, ship building, and musical instruments.

1 The Last Frontier

The famous explorer John Muir called Alaska a "picture of icy wildness," and though he wrote those words more than a century ago, they still ring true today. From the Arctic Ocean to snow-covered Mount Denali, Alaska is a land of natural wonders. Even the name of the state honors its size and importance: *Alaska* comes from the native Aleut people's word *Alyeshka*, meaning "the great land." Without a doubt, Alaska is great in its rugged beauty, size, wilderness, and people.

From Mountains to the Sea

Alaska is the largest of all fifty states in the nation, covering more than 570,000 square miles with more than 33,000 miles of shoreline. Within this remarkable area of land lies an amazing array of mountains, rivers, glaciers, volcanoes, islands, tundra, and rainforests. Two oceans, the Arctic and the North Pacific, and three seas, the Bering, Chukchi, and Beaufort, surround the state on three sides. Alaska has more

Alaska's Borders
North: Arctic Ocean
South: Gulf of Alaska, Pacific Ocean, and Canada
East: Canada
West: Bering Sea

Bright fireweed blooms in Brotherhood Park in southeastern Alaska. Beyond the plants are a glacier and the Coast Mountains.

Alaska

than three million lakes and several major rivers, among them the Copper River and the Yukon. Huge coastal mountain ranges in the east and southeast rise up from sea level. To the north, the remote Brooks Range is the northernmost tip of the Rocky Mountains. Permanently frozen earth, ice floes and icebergs, eerie Northern Lights, days when the sun shines at midnight, and more are all part of Alaska's fantastic glory.

The Southern Coast

Alaska can be divided into several natural regions. The southern coastal region of Alaska is often divided into two sections: southeastern and south-central. Southeastern Alaska—sometimes called the panhandle—is a narrow, mountainous region stretching toward, but not reaching, the rest of the lower forty-eight states. Thick rain forests of Sitka spruce, hemlock, Ponderosa pine, and Western cedar cover the mountains of the panhandle. A group of 1,100 offshore islands creates a system of canals, fjords, and channels called the Inside Passage. Cruise ships, ferries, tankers, tugs, barges, container ships, and pleasure boats travel through these scenic and protected waterways. Southeastern Alaska is generally warmer and wetter than the rest of the state. Most years, 150 to 200 inches of rain or snow will fall in the area.

The climate of the Alaskan rain-forests is so warm and humid that moss grows on the trunks of the spruce and hemlock trees.

On the upper slopes of the mountains, snow falls year round. Rivers freeze and form glaciers that flow to the sea.

There are more than 100,000 glaciers in Alaska. The largest, the Malaspina Glacier, covers about 1,500 square miles.

If you were to travel the Inside Passage, you would begin in the rainforests near the Misty Fjords National Monument. There, fog floats over narrow seas and steep cliffs. You would end your journey surrounded by icebergs and glaciers in the Glacier Bay National Park. In geologic time, Glacier Bay is very new. Just slightly more than two hundred years ago, when British captain George Vancouver first sailed the area, he saw only "compact solid mountains of ice." Today, the glacier has melted to form a bay sixty-five miles long. Tongass National Forest, the country's largest national forest, is located beyond Glacier Bay.

More than half of the state's population lives in south-central Alaska, where you will find snow-covered mountain ranges, seas bursting with marine life, busy fishing communities, farmlands, national parks, and the state's largest city, Anchorage. Huge amounts of precipitation fall, forming vast areas of glaciers, ice, and snow. One glacier, the Bering, is larger than the entire state of Rhode Island.

Alaska has many national parks. Wrangell-St. Elias National Park, the United States' largest national park, is located in south-central Alaska. Inside the park, the St. Elias Mountains link with the Wrangell, Alaska, and Chugach mountain ranges. Grizzly bears, mountain goats, Dall sheep, bison, and other wild creatures roam the 13.2-million-acre park. The smallest of Alaska's eight national parks, Kenai Fjords, is on the Kenai Peninsula.

A boat moves through Cook Inlet, with Anchorage and the Chugach Mountains beyond.

There, more than 400 inches of snow fall each year on mountains, glaciers, and a 300-square-mile sheet of ice called the Harding Icefield. Along this peninsula, fjords and the Gulf of Alaska are home to whales, seals, otters, and sea lions, as well as puffins, murres, and other seabirds. Hardy mammals such as mountain goats, moose, bears, wolverines, and marmots live near the edges of the icefield.

The Pacific Ocean borders parts of Alaska. The state is included in the Pacific Rim of Fire, which is where many of the world's most active volcanoes are located.

Western Alaska

Western Alaska is an amazing region rich in wildlife. There are six national wildlife refuges in this area. One stretches across Kodiak Island and its island group. This is the only place in the world where you will find the Kodiak brown bear, the largest grizzly (or brown) bear in the world. Other remote wildlife refuges are on the Aleutian and Pribilof Islands. As many as 30 million seabirds migrate through the area. These birds include Emperor geese, murres, kittiwakes, cormorants, auklets, and puffins.

The Aleutian Islands—a string of treeless, windswept islands—stretch 1200 miles across the icy Bering Sea, toward Russia. After leaving Dutch Harbor, a busy Aleutian fishing port, mariners sail over waters brimming with killer whales, grey whales, all five species of Pacific salmon, Steller's sea lions, and porpoises. Many of the Aleutian Mountains are actively

Fierce winds called *williwaws* build up on one side of the Aleutian Mountains, spill over the top, and race down the other side. Raging up to 125 miles per hour, williwaws can sink ships and make birds fly backward.

volcanic, such as those in the region called the Valley of Ten Thousand Smokes.

The 19-million-acre Yukon Delta National Wildlife Refuge in northwest Alaska is the largest wildlife refuge in the world. Across a broad plain flow two of Alaska's greatest rivers, the Yukon—the state's longest river—and the Kuskokwim. Both rivers spill into the sea and form enormous deltas. A delta is a network of streams, inlets, and deposits of rock and sediment. The area has more than 40,000 lakes. It is a watery wonderland for waterfowl. North of the delta, the Seward Peninsula juts westward across the Bering Strait, ending 56 miles from Siberia in eastern Russia. The historic village of Nome rests on the southern coast of the peninsula and overlooks Norton Sound. On the north side of the peninsula, lava beds, soaring sea cliffs, lagoons, and hot springs are home to waterfowl and birds of prey such as bald eagles, hawks, falcons, and owls.

The Yukon River is the third longest river highway in North America. Much of it can be navigated when it is not frozen over.

The Interior

The area of Alaska called the Interior is immense. The eastern edge of the region begins at the Canadian border and then sweeps west to the Yukon Delta. It is bordered to the south by the Alaska Range and to the north by the Brooks Range.

The central part of the Interior is mostly tundra, a landform that is flat, treeless, and cold. Great rivers run their courses through the Interior, among them the Yukon, the Kuskokwin, Tanana, Porcupine, Koyukuk, and Innoko Rivers. The Tanana flows past Fairbanks, the region's major city. In the Interior's wilderness areas, salmon swim up rivers to breed, and giant trumpeter swans and rare sandhill cranes spend summers raising their young. Creatures such as caribou, moose, grizzly, lynx, and wolf make their homes on the tundra, throughout the mountain ranges, or in forests of birch, spruce, and aspen.

One of the most extraordinary places in the world is in Alaska's Interior. Mount McKinley, the tallest point in North America, towers over the other mountains in the Alaska Range. Alaskans call the peak by its native Athabaskan name, Denali, which means "the Great One," or "the High One." At 20,320 feet, Denali can be seen two hundred miles away.

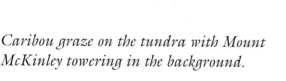

Caribou graze on the tundra with Mount McKinley towering in the background.

The Arctic North

At first, northern Alaska may seem cold and bleak, but it is full of life. Lying north of the Arctic Circle, the Brooks Range runs east to west across the southern border of Alaska's arctic region. The range is the northern tip of the continental divide and contains two national parks, Kobuk Valley and Gates of the Arctic. The peaks are jagged. "They go straight up and then straight down, like shark's teeth," says one truck driver, "and then it's flat all the way to the sea." Rivers that flow from the Brooks Range are some of the wildest and most unspoiled in the world.

Trees, such as spruce, fir, and pine grow on the south slope of the range. Because an average of only six to ten inches of precipitation falls each year on the north side, the north slope and

Almost 40 miles north of the Arctic Circle is Alaska's Kobuk Valley National Park. The Great Kobuk Sand Dunes are located within the park. The sand was brought to the region by glaciers, wind, and water.

arctic coastal plain are nearly barren of trees. Instead, scrubby shrubs, mosses, wildflowers, and lichens grow on Alaska's arctic tundra. Trees are unable to take root because underneath the surface soil of the tundra is a layer of permafrost, or permanently frozen earth. Permafrost cannot hold water, so plants with root systems starve. When the short arctic spring comes, the snow and ice melt, and pools of water form above the permafrost layer.

Wildflowers and grasses burst forth. Musk oxen, grizzly bears, foxes, wolves, and caribou, as well as birds from all over the world move about the tundra in spring and summer and feast on the wildlife. Along the coastline, rare marine mammals live among ice floes and along the coastal plain. These include Pacific walrus, bearded, ringed, and spotted seals, polar bears, beluga and gray whales, killer whales, and harbor porpoises.

Climate and Seasons

The coldest temperature ever recorded in the United States (minus 80 degrees Fahrenheit) was measured at Prospect Creek Camp in the Brooks Range in 1971. But the weather in Alaska varies quite a bit. The Pacific Ocean warms the southeast and south-central regions, and the Alaska Range blocks many cold, northerly winds, so temperatures are much milder there than in the rest of the state. These temperatures range from around 20 degrees to 60 degrees Fahrenheit. Like the Aleutian Islands, the southern coastal areas are very wet. But the Aleutian Islands are colder, and the skies overhead are gray and cloudy on an average of 355 days a year.

Seventy inches of snow often falls on Anchorage each year, while the nearby Chugach Mountains get more than 500 inches. Surrounded by mountain ranges, Alaska's Interior has the most contrasting weather changes. In summer, long days and sunny skies raise temperatures sometimes into the 90s. In winter, when days average only four hours of light, the temperature can drop to minus 60 degrees. Only twelve inches of precipitation fall in the Interior, but when it falls as snow, it stays on the ground for most of the winter. In the arctic region, even less precipitation falls, and scientists call the area a frozen desert.

Winter snow blankets Unalaska Island—part of the Aleutian Islands.

In winter, the Arctic Ocean ices over, as do the rivers flowing across the tundra. For nine months of the year, a massive sheet of ice blankets the region. Winds sail across this frosty plain, where winter temperatures average minus 20 degrees Fahrenheit. Added wind chills can make the air temperature feel like minus 60 degrees or lower. Even in summer, the arctic north is rarely above 50 degrees Fahrenheit.

You cannot ski on the snow in Alaska when it is too cold. At 40 degrees below zero, there is not enough warmth for skis to glide across the surface of the dry snow.

In Alaska, the summer solstice, or the longest day of the year, and the winter solstice, or the shortest day of the year, are more than just dates on the calendar. The Arctic Circle passes through the region. This is the distance from the North Pole that marks the points where the sun does not set during the summer solstice and does not rise during the winter solstice. In the Alaskan village of Barrow, north of the Arctic Circle, the summer sun stays in the sky, day and night, for 84 days. Below the Arctic Circle, summer days are also quite long. In Anchorage for example, the sun sets well after 10 p.m., on most summer nights. Alaskans love their long, light-filled days. "In the summer, you just go, go, go, go! You have so much energy, you don't want to sleep," laughs an Anchorage woman. But winter days are another story. For 67 days in winter, Barrow is without daylight. One native says, "They say that if you make it through an Alaskan winter, you deserve an Alaskan summer."

Spring in Alaska is big news. The season, like autumn, is very short, but when it arrives, it arrives with a bang. Along the Arctic coastline, the sea ice melts and splits into pieces called pack ice. These large ice floes form the main hunting ground for polar bears. Elsewhere in Alaska, melting snow builds up huge amounts of slush and mud. Frozen rivers crack and thaw, sending water and chunks of ice downstream. Alaskans call the season "break up."

Spring and autumn are the best times of year to look for the aurora borealis, also known as the Northern Lights. This amazing event happens when electrically charged particles from the sun crash into the polar regions of the Earth's atmosphere. The gases in the atmosphere react by flashing colored beams of light across the northern sky.

The spectacular Northern Lights glow above this farm in the Matanuska Valley.

In the Wild

There are more wild caribou living in Alaska than there are people. Alaska's wilderness is a refuge for millions of wild creatures. Besides caribou, there are animals that are quite common in Alaska but rare in the rest of the United States, such as wolves, musk oxen, Dall sheep, sea otters, river otters, loons, snowy owls, and trumpeter swans. Some animals that are threatened or endangered in the lower forty-eight states are thriving in Alaska. These include the bald eagle, gray wolf, grizzly bear, wolverine, and lynx. Migratory birds, such as the arctic tern—which flies all the way from the South Pole each year—visit Alaska every summer to nest and feed. The clean waters of the state are rich habitats for sea life such as walrus, Pacific salmon, king crab, beluga, humpback and gray whales, many types of seals, and polar bears.

Horned puffins nest in rocky cliffs near Alaska's chilly coastal waters.

Plants & Animals

Polar Bear

Polar bears live in the arctic region of Alaska's coast. They spend so much time in the water that they are classified as a marine mammal and not a land mammal. Polar bears can swim for hundreds of miles. With a keen sense of smell, sharp claws, strength, speed, and the camouflage of a white coat, a polar bear is a successful hunter of seals, walruses, whales, and birds.

Walrus

Walruses live in shallow waters near land or on the ice along Alaska's coast. These large marine mammals weigh a ton or more and have long canine teeth that resemble tusks. Walruses use these tusks to crack breathing holes in ice, attack predators such as bears, and help pull their huge bodies out of the water.

Snowy Owl

Year round, snowy owls live on the open tundra. These large birds of prey nest on the ground and hunt in the snow and over grassy meadows and marshlands. They mainly eat rodents, hares, songbirds, geese, and sometimes weasels and foxes.

Caribou

Caribou are perfectly adapted to living on the tundra. Their hooves work like snowshoes in the snow. The hooves also help them swim and dig for food and when the snow melts, the hooves keep the heavy animals from sinking into the mud. Both male and female caribou grow antlers, which they shed each year. During spring and summer, caribou munch on the leaves of plants such as willows, sedges, and blueberries, and in winter they eat reindeer lichen.

Reindeer Lichen

Reindeer lichen is a gray-green plant that grows across Alaska's vast tundra. Lichens are really two plants (fungi and algae) joined together. Lichens do not have roots and do not need soil to grow. To survive, the fungus part of the plant takes water out of the air, and the algae part makes energy from sunlight. Reindeer lichen is a favorite food for caribou, reindeer, musk oxen, and moose.

Monkshood

Monkshood is a leafy wildflower with a blue, hood-shaped flower. A member of the buttercup family, the plant grows near marshes and springs. If eaten, all parts of this plant are poisonous. Monkshood was once known as wolf's bane and was used by hunters to bait and trap wolves.

Yet even with Alaska's small population and vast areas of untouched wilderness, there are still threatened or endangered species in the state. Birds such as the short-tailed albatross, the American peregrine falcon, and the Eskimo curlew are in danger of being lost forever. Due to hunting, fishing, and pollution, marine mammals such as the Steller's sea lion, harbor seals, and bowhead and humpback whales are also at risk.

In one international effort, Alaskans are making a difference. The short-tailed albatross makes its home in Japan but flies as far as Alaska to feed in its rich arctic waters. There were once millions of these giant seabirds, but now only a few remain on Earth. In the 1800s, the albatross was a familiar sight to Alaskan fishermen, but in this century the fishermen rarely see the bird flying over their boats. But when they do, there has been trouble. As fishermen toss their fishing lines and hooks overboard, the birds dive for the bait and often get tangled in the lines. Fish hooks can also snag the birds. Fishermen do not mean to harm the birds, especially those so rare. Recently, Alaskan fishermen have begun to follow new laws to help save this endangered species. Instead of dropping their baited hooks in the water as they always have done, fishermen now attach noisy streamers to the gear to scare the birds away. Though doing so costs the fishermen more time and money, they play their part to help save a rare bird. Alaskans know they have a special place in the world, and they act to protect their wild lands for wildlife.

Steller's sea lions weigh about 50 pounds at birth. Adult males may weigh over 1,000 pounds and adult females may reach nearly 600 pounds.

The Last Frontier

2 From the Beginning

Alaska's history is as colorful as the wildflowers that bloom on the tundra after "break up" in the spring. Few states can claim a past as wild and extreme. In spite of being one of the newest states in the Union, Alaska has a long and amazing saga of ancient peoples and cultures, strong traditions, hardy explorers, and daring adventurers.

People of the Land Bridge

When part of the land known as North America was covered under Ice Age glaciers, the level of the sea was lower than today. About 10,000 to 30,000 years ago, scientists say, there was no Bering Strait. Instead there was a wide land bridge between the continents of Asia and North America. Scientists call the area Beringia. Prehistoric people walked over this bridge, following musk oxen, mammoths, mastodons, and other big game. In time, these hunters migrated from Asia to North and South America. A few groups stayed in the region, and they are the ancestors of people living in Alaska today.

These Eskimo children pose for a picture near Nome around 1911.

When the Ice Age ended, the level of the sea rose and flooded the land bridge.

The Alaska state fossil is the woolly mammoth, the largest member of the elephant family. Now extinct for 11,000 years, the wooly mammoth once fed on tundra grasses.

The first people of Alaska can be traced to three main groups: Eskimo, Aleut, and Athabascan Indian. Two Eskimo groups settled in Alaska, the Inupiat and the Yup'ik. The Inupiat settled along the arctic coastline. Men carved tools and hunting spears from ivory and bone. They fished, hunted waterfowl, and caught seals using narrow kayaks made from bone and hides. To capture whales and large ivory-tusked walrus, men joined in hunting parties and used bigger, wider boats. Women and girls prepared food, made clothing, and tended their dwellings. Their homes were made of whale bones and hides, driftwood, or snow. Often the community built a winter earth lodge for ceremonies. With little wood to use for fuel, the Eskimos burned seal oil. Living along Norton Sound, the Yup'ik Eskimos enjoyed a milder climate. They fished using hooks, spears, and nets and also hunted ducks and birds.

The earliest Aleuts, relatives of the Eskimos, settled on the Aleutian Islands and formed a society rich in art, religion, and community life. The Aleutian Islands lie between the Bering Sea and the North Pacific. The climate was foggy, windy, and harsh. Yet, the area did not freeze over and food was plentiful. Men and boys fished with hooks and line and went to sea in kayaks. Men made sleek kayaks of bone and skins and carved beautiful tools and weapons made from bone and ivory. Using harpoons, they hunted sea otters, hair seals, and sea lions. On land, the women, children, and old men gathered berries and roots. They also walked the beaches collecting mussels, clams, sea urchins, kelp, and seaweed. Millions of birds migrate through the islands, and their eggs were an important food. Whole families of parents, children, aunts, uncles, cousins, and grandparents lived together in houses built underground. The women wove baskets and sewed sealskins into waterproof clothing.

Early Natives living in Alaska's cold climates made clothing out of fur to keep warm.

While most of the Athabascan people migrated inland to Alaska's Interior, three tribes settled on the panhandle: the Haida, Tlinget, and Tsimshian. These Native Americans belonged to a group now called the Northwest Coast Native Americans. They shared a culture with tribes living along the coasts of what is now western Canada and Washington state. Like the Aleuts, their weather was mild year round, but unlike the Aleuts, they had forests—lush rain forests—from which they cut wood to make houses, carvings, tools, and boats. The Northwest Coast Native Americans were blessed with a surplus of food. Rivers and seas were filled with wild salmon. The men fished using dip-nets, hooks, and line. Their boats were dugout canoes. Each canoe was carved out of a single, large tree. The women gathered berries and roots.

Ceremonies and feasts were colorful events. Craftsmen carved and painted masks, and women wove decorative baskets and sewed fancy garments fashioned from seeds, beads, shells, and feathers. The men were also great warriors, and often went out to sea to raid rival villages.

The inland Athabascan people were nomadic, meaning that they moved from place to place, usually to follow herds of caribou, moose, or other game. They made stone tools and weapons. In summer, the people lived in houses of bark that were easy to break down and carry away. During the warmer time of year, they hunted game and caught salmon and freshwater fish. In the forests, they tracked deer and elk and gathered berries. To prepare for the long, cold winters, the people prepared large amounts of meat and moved into underground shelters.

Athabascans who followed herds might have lived in domed huts made of branches and animal hides.

Europeans Come Ashore

As Native Alaskans prospered in their remote part of the world, the rest of humanity knew little or nothing about them. But that ended in 1741, when a Danish sea captain named Vitus Bering led a crew and two ships to the "land to the north." Sailing under orders from the Russian government, Bering and his men faced sickness and hardship. But they reached the Aleutian islands and the west coast of Alaska and found great natural riches. Captain Bering and twenty members of his crew died while trying to return to Russia. But survivors of the passage returned home bringing sea otter pelts and news that the area was bursting with fur-bearing animals.

The Bering Strait and the Bering Sea were named after Vitus Bering. The Steller's sea lion and the Steller's jay, as well as the extinct Steller's sea cow, are named for Georg Steller, a scientist aboard Bering's ship.

This hand-colored woodcut shows an artist's version of Bering's ships wrecking on the Aleutian Islands in 1741.

The fur trade was very important to Russia's economy, and a Russian fur trader could earn three times his normal yearly wage with a single Alaskan sea otter pelt. So, Russian fur trappers and traders quickly set sail for Alaska and began trading with the Native people. By the late 1700s, Russia was the greatest fur-trading empire in the world. In the beginning, the Natives were eager to trade with the Russians for useful tools made of iron and other goods. Many of the first Russian traders had Native wives and families. But soon, serious problems came about. Without meaning to, the Russians carried diseases that sickened and killed many Natives. Large Russian fur companies formed settlements in Sitka and on Kodiak Island. Out of greed for sea otter pelts, the fur companies treated the Natives harshly. They forced the Aleuts to hunt sea otters as far from home as California. By the 1820s, nearly all the sea otters along the coast were killed off. And Native Alaskans were suffering.

Near the present-day town of Sitka, the Russians established their main colony and most powerful fur company, the Russian-America Company. This company was granted rights by the Russian ruler to "all industries connected with the capture of wild animals and all fishing industries on the shore of Northwestern America." The Russians tried to keep their activities in Alaska a secret from other nations.

In the years between 1774 and 1793, Spain sent thirteen ships to Alaska to study the Pacific coastline. The Spanish never set up a colony, but they mapped much of the area and left behind many Spanish place names, such as Malaspina Glacier, the port of Valdez, and Madre de Dios Island. Soon after, explorers from Britain, France, and the United States started to take notice.

During the eighteenth century, Captain Cook and his ships sailed across the world's oceans a record three times.

British explorer Captain James Cook sailed into Alaskan waters in May 1778, hoping to find a northern shipping route between the Pacific and Atlantic Oceans. Before leaving the area, he carefully mapped much of the Alaskan coastline. He and his crew also carried away sea otter pelts. The crew made a hefty profit selling the pelts in Chinese ports.

Word about Alaska spread around the world, and more ships arrived. One ship was guided by British explorer George Vancouver. He mapped the Inside Passage and was the first European to spy "distant, stupendous mountains covered with snow." He was describing the landforms that are now known as Mount McKinley and the Alaskan Range.

Seward's Folly

American fur traders competed with the Russian-America Company, and relations between the nations were poor. The Americans traded sugar, guns, and alcohol to the Native Alaskans. These items upset traditional ways. Some of the Native groups used the guns to fight against the Russians.

The first Russian governor of Alaska, Alexander Baranov, said that because of some of these troubles Alaska made him "old before his time."

By 1835, American whaling ships based in New England were pursuing the right to hunt whale as far away as Alaska. While hunting in the arctic, New England whalers met Eskimo whale hunters and learned about hunting the bowhead whale. These whalers found that they could get more oil from bowheads. Whaling ships flocked to the region. Before the discovery of petroleum in 1859, whale oil was an important fuel used in the United States. New England whalers were the major suppliers. So in 1865, near the end of the American Civil War, the southern Confederacy planned to destroy the Union's whaling fleet. It sent the warship *Shenandoah* into the Pacific Ocean to hunt down the American whalers. In the Bering Strait alone, twenty whaling ships were sunk. The attacks made it clear that Russia was unable to protect Alaska.

Russia also had growing money troubles. They had lost a costly war with Britain and sea otters were going extinct, making the fur trade harder to support. By 1865, Russian rulers started to believe that a good way to help their economy was to sell Alaska to the Americans. President Andrew Johnson's secretary of state, William Seward, believed in Alaska. He wanted to purchase it from Russia. Many thought he was wrong. People called the idea of buying Alaska, "Seward's Folly" (a folly is a foolish act), "Seward's Ice Box," or "Johnson's Polar Bear Garden." Yet, in 1867, the deal was struck. The United States bought the Russian colony of Alaska for $7.2 million, or about 2.5 cents per acre.

Try Your Hand at Scrimshaw

Scrimshaw is an art form practiced by Native Alaskans who taught it to American whalers in the 1800s. The craftspeople scratched or etched fine designs onto ivory or bone, and colored the designs with dark ink.

What You Need
Solid white plastic (a yogurt or margarine lid)
A cutting board
A sharp nail or long wood screw
Black acrylic paint
A paint rag
A pen

Select a picture or design from books, magazines, the Internet, or create your own. Using the pen, draw your design onto the plastic.

Place the plastic on the cutting board and use the nail or screw to scratch the design into the plastic. The tip of the nail or screw is very sharp so be very careful. You can ask an adult to help you with the scratching part of the project.

When you are ready to color your scrimshaw, place a drop of paint on the surface and rub it into the scratches. Clean the surface with the rag. When the surface is dry, you can add more details to your design and repeat the process.

Gold Rush

For many residents, everyday life in Alaska did not change much after the United States bought the land. Americans arrived slowly. Small military installations were sent to the region to act as government. American missionaries visited and reported back to Washington, D.C. that Alaskans needed a civic government and public schools. The naturalist John Muir toured Alaska and wrote about the beauty of the Inside Passage and Glacier Bay, calling it a "fairyland." Tourists anxious to see the wonders of the new territory boarded cruise ships and set sail. But it took the discovery of gold to convince most Americans to come to Alaska.

From the 1880s to the early 1900s, gold was discovered in many Alaskan locations. Once a discovery was made, American miners, homesteaders, merchants, and real estate dealers streamed into towns such as Sitka, Nome, Juneau, and Fairbanks. One of the largest gold strikes in the region was along the Klondike River in Canada. To get to the site, many fortune hunters sailed the Inside Passage from Seattle, Washington, to Skagway, Alaska. Car-

rying a year's worth of food, clothing, and supplies, the miners then began a steep and dangerous trek over the St. Elias Mountains. The Skagway newspaper reported, "Miners in the Yukon require strong and rich food and they will drink bacon grease like so much water." More than 60,000 Americans

Gold miners heading to the Klondike set out on the Dyea Trail—also called the Chilkoot Trail—in 1898.

traveled across Alaska during the gold rush, and many of them decided to stay.

Penniless miners in Nome could not believe their good luck when they realized that the sand along the beaches of the Bering Sea was mixed with gold. No one needed an official claim to shovel up the gold since the beaches belonged to everybody.

Statehood and Beyond

In the early decades of the twentieth century, many of Alaska's disorderly mining and fishing camps grew into towns. Fur trading became less important, while gold and copper mining, logging, and fishing created jobs for Alaskan workers. Roads, railroads, ships, riverboats, and telegraph lines were built to connect Alaska to the outside world. Margaret Murie, an Alaskan author, described her childhood in Fairbanks: "We were all far away from the rest of the world; we had to depend on one another." On August 24, 1912, Alaska officially became a territory.

In 1917, the United States was involved in World War I, and many Alaskan residents joined the military. After the war, in 1922, Roy Jones, a former World War I pilot, flew a small floatplane from Seattle to Ketchikan. This floatplane had structures that allowed it to float once it landed in water. In a land where travel is so difficult and bridges and roads are so few, this flight was an important event. Soon, small airplanes, many fitted with floats to land on water, delivered mail and other goods throughout all of Alaska.

Remote areas are called the "bush" in Alaska, and bush pilots made living in the wilderness easier. But before air travel, dog sled was the most common means of traveling rugged, roadless areas. In 1925, the village of Nome was fighting an outbreak of a serious disease called diphtheria. Supplies of a vaccine to prevent the disease were very low. A doctor in Nome telegraphed for help.

With the help of Alaskan Natives, this doctor used a dog sled to bring small pox medicine to remote villages.

In Anchorage a doctor arranged to have twenty mushers and their dog sled teams relay the vaccine to Nome. The temperature was 35 degrees below zero, but the twenty mushers relayed the medicine to each other across 674 miles in five days and seven and a half hours. Nome was spared, and to this day, a dog sled race called the Iditarod is held in honor of the event. The word *Iditarod* comes from a Native Athabascan word meaning "a distant place."

During the 1930s, Alaska remained a "distant place" to many Americans living in the lower forty-eight states. But when World War II began, Alaska became very important as a military site. Alaska became known to many as the Guardian of the North. President Roosevelt ordered fuel pipelines, airfields, military bases, and roads to be built. The Alaska-Canada Highway was built, and today it is sometimes called the Alcan Highway. Many miners, engineers, soldiers, construction workers, and others moved to Alaska.

In 1942, Japan invaded Dutch Harbor in the Aleutian Islands. Many battles were fought before American forces overcame the Japanese army in Alaska in 1943. A few years after the war ended, the United States and Russia became rival nations, and Alaska, being so close to Russia, was very important to

On June 3, 1932, Japanese forces bombed military outposts in Dutch Harbor.

the U.S. military. As new roads, pipelines, docks, railroads, and airports were built, Alaska boomed. Families joined the workers, and soon there were new houses, churches, and schools. On January 3, 1959, President Eisenhower officially admitted Alaska to the Union as the forty-ninth state.

Oil and Water

Once Alaska became a state, citizens set out to create a steady economy and government. Logging, fishing, mining, and tourism were the major industries. In 1968, oil and gas were discovered on the North slope, and a large part of Alaska was transformed. In 1977, an 800-mile pipeline, called the Trans-Alaska Pipeline, was constructed to carry oil from Prudhoe Bay to the port of Valdez on Prince William Sound. Thousands of people moved to the region to work in the oilfields and on the pipeline. The state grew wealthy selling its oil.

In 1980, an important law was passed that protected more than 100 million acres of Alaskan wilderness. Part of the wilderness was spoiled in 1989, when a tanker named the *Exxon Valdez* ran aground and spilled 11 million gallons of its oily cargo into the clean, clear waters of Prince William Sound. Damage from this disaster continues to this day. Some animals, such as river otter, bald eagles, and salmon, recovered. Others, such as loons, harbor seals, and Pacific herring, have not fared well.

At the start of the twenty-first century, certain government and industry leaders want to drill for oil in the Arctic National Wildlife Refuge (ANWR). Some Alaskans support the idea,

believing that the profits will help the economy. Others think that the landscape and wildlife will be ruined forever. Alaska governor Frank Murkowski once said, "Some of our choices are easy, others very tough." Today, citizens of the forty-ninth state face many challenges as they balance the need for jobs and trade with the care needed for its extraordinary natural wealth.

Oil spills have killed and injured many animals, hurt the fragile balance of the ecosystems, and cost millions of dollars in clean-up measures.

Alaska

Important Dates

12,000 B.C.E.–7000 B.C.E.   Ancestors of Athabascan Native Americans cross the land bridge from Siberia.

7000 B.C.E.–4000 B.C.E.   Ancestors of Aleuts and Eskimos cross over the Bering land bridge and settle in Alaska.

1728   Vitus Bering leads an expedition to Alaska.

1776   Captain James Cook sails Alaskan waters, seeking the Northwest Passage.

1799   Alexander Baranov establishes Old Sitka and oversees the Russian-American Company.

1867   The United States purchases Alaska from Russia.

1897-1900   Many prospectors, explorers, and businesspeople move to Alaska during the Klondike Gold Rush.

William Seward

1912   Alaska becomes a territory.

1942   Japan bombs Dutch Harbor.

1959   Alaska becomes the forty-ninth state on January 3.

1968   Oil is pumped from a well at Prudhoe Bay and helps oil to become one of the most important parts of Alaska's economy.

1971   Alaska Native Claims Settlement Act is signed into law, granting Natives rights to ancestral lands.

1977   The Trans-Alaska Pipeline is completed from Prudhoe Bay to Valdez.

1989   The *Exxon Valdez* spills 11 million gallons of crude oil into Prince William Sound.

1992   Mount Spurr, an active volcano near Anchorage erupts, covering the city in ash.

The Exxon Valdez tanker

1997   The twelve-billionth barrel of oil reaches the port of Valdez.

2003   U.S. Congress votes no to oil drilling in the Arctic National Wildlife Refuge.

3 The People

Alaska is the largest state, yet only a small number of people live within its borders. But having the third smallest population in the country does not stop citizens from having an amazingly large variety of cultures and lifestyles. To Alaskans, home can be such a satisfying place that many citizens never cross the state line. Many that do say that they are going "Outside." As one Anchorage woman reveals, "We have a saying, 'Never come to Alaska while you are young, or you will forever spoil your eyes for the rest of the world!'" Alaskans are pleased to be Alaskans, and few would care to live anywhere else.

> When the word *Native* is spelled with a capital *N*, it refers to Alaska's first people: Aleut, Eskimo, or Athabascan people. When *native* is spelled with a lower-case *n*, it refers to any citizen born in the state.

Native Alaskans

There are nearly 100,000 Alaska Natives. They are 16 percent of the population of Alaska. Many live and work in cities such as Anchorage and Fairbanks, but many more live in rural

A brother and sister living in the northern town of Barrow wear traditional parkas.

An Eskimo woman living in present-day Barrow tans hides like her ancestors did.

villages and settlements. Hundreds of Native villages are small and quite remote. Most can only be reached by boat or airplane. Many village residents practice what is called a subsistence lifestyle. They hunt, trap, gather, or grow their own food and barter for goods and services like their ancestors did. These Natives also trap furs to make clothing, fashion tools, fishnets, and boats, and create art with materials they collect.

However, in the past several decades, great changes have happened to the traditional lifestyle. Hunters use guns rather than harpoons, villagers travel by snow-machine instead of dog sled, and fishermen drive aluminum boats with outboard motors instead of paddling kayaks. Even the most remote villages have televisions, telephones, and connections to the Internet.

The Tsimshian tribe on Annette Island is the only Native American reservation in Alaska. The tribe controls fishing and taxes, and also has its own court system, including a tribal court, juvenile court, and appeals court.

Despite modern conveniences, village life is tough. People want better schools, health care, updated services, and store-bought goods. There are very few year-round jobs, so it is difficult for residents to pay for these improvements. Some say the old ways are better but are being forgotten. As one Yup'ik elder lamented, "Parents are losing their traditional parenting skills.

They need to know how to teach children respect for the people around us and for our environment." But village schools play a central role in the community. "Our kids participate in all the extracurricular activities," reports a Yup'ik village school principal named Harley Sundown. "They play basketball, race cross-country, and compete in the Native Youth Olympics. We even have a radio station!" Village schools also teach traditional culture. Sundown explains, "We are still pretty much culturally rich. We teach subsistence classes in school. It's very hands-on. The kids learn trap-building, net-making, boat building, all the traditional stuff you can think of!" Besides schools, there are community programs sponsored by the Native corporations throughout Alaskan villages that coach children in traditional arts and crafts such as dance, song, and storytelling, blanket-weaving, basket-making, kayak-building, wood and ivory carving, and beadwork.

Fishing is a family affair in Native villages. Men and boys set the nets and catch the fish. Small children gather driftwood for fires. Women and girls cut the fish, set it on the rooftops to dry, then smoke and store the fish for winter. As one Native community leader says, "What we eat is who we are."

Schoolchildren play on their school's playground in the Aleutian Islands.

Northward Bound

Immigrants have always come to Alaska looking for better opportunities. The first European immigrants to move to Alaska were Russians who planned to set up a post for trading furs. They built several outposts and soon the Russian Tsar (the ruler) sent missionaries to convert the Natives to the Russian Orthodox Church. They also set

Young women living in Sitka dress in traditional Russian clothing for a cultural celebration.

up schools for Native and Non-Native children. Many of these schools continued into the twentieth century. Throughout the southern coast of Alaska, especially in Sitka, you will find Russian-style buildings and domed churches filled with gold artwork. Numerous family and town names are Russian, and many Alaskans are faithful to the Russian Orthodox Church.

The next wave of arrivals came in the mid 1800s. News of gold spread around the world, and Alaska-bound fortune hunters arrived. They came from the United States, Canada, Italy, Sweden, Norway, Japan, China, and France. Each discovery of gold in Alaska brought hundreds and then thousands of people to remote and uncharted areas. When others followed to trade with the gold miners, the camps turned into boomtowns. The challenges that these newcomers faced were enormous. But their ability

The old-time prospectors were called "sourdoughs." This name was given because they used a sourdough yeast mixture to help their camp bread rise. Today, many long-time Alaskans are proud to be called "sourdoughs."

Alaska

to endure disappointment, sickness, hunger, bitter cold, storms, floods, and countless other hardships remains a source of pride to their descendants today.

Commercial fishing started another population boom in Alaska near the end of the nineteenth century. Fishermen and cannery workers moved to the Kenai Peninsula and established the first factories in Alaska. As forts were established, American soldiers came and went. In the 1940s, the military set up permanent bases, and soldiers and their families became Alaska residents.

The greatest boom of all for Alaska was the discovery of oil. From the 1950s to the 1980s, oilfield and construction jobs lured thousands north. By the end of the twentieth century, the oil and mining booms were over, but many of the people decided to stay on. The population of Anchorage had grown to more than 260,000 people. This was twice the population of the entire state just fifty years earlier. In cities and towns around the state, Caucasians—or whites—make up 69 percent of the total population. African Americans represent 3 percent,

Asian Americans 4 percent, and Latinos 4 percent. In many of the remote villages, Native Alaskans are the majority members of the population.

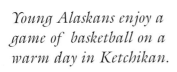

Young Alaskans enjoy a game of basketball on a warm day in Ketchikan.

Famous Alaskans

Leonhard Seppala: Serum Run Hero

In the early 1900s, Leonhard Seppala worked as a miner, but found happiness as a sled dog trainer and musher. In 1925, Seppala was part of a special crew of mushers who delivered life-saving medicine to the arctic town of Nome. Seppala and his team raced farther than any other musher—260 miles in minus 30 degree weather. Today, the famous Iditarod sled dog race is run in honor of Seppala and the other brave mushers and dogs that came to the aid of the people of Nome.

Jewel: Singer and Songwriter

Singer Jewel Kilcher grew up in Anchorage and later, Homer, Alaska. Jewel says that the Alaskan wilderness is her greatest inspiration. She not only sings, but writes songs, yodels, and publishes poetry. She has won many awards for her music and has performed all over the world.

Libby Riddles: Dog Trainer and Musher

At age 17, Libby Riddles built a cabin in the wilderness and adopted sled dogs. In 1978, she began training the sled dogs for racing. In 1985, Riddles competed in the Iditarod race. When a blizzard kept most competitors inside, she decided to mush ahead into the stormy night. As a result, she was the first to cross the finish line and became the first woman to win the Iditarod. Today, she writes about her experiences and trains sled dogs in Homer, Alaska.

Elizabeth Peratrovich: Activist

Elizabeth Peratrovich was born in 1911, in the small coastal town of Petersburg. She was a Tlingit who was adopted by white Protestant missionaries. As an adult, she moved to Juneau and was horrified by signs that said, "No Natives Allowed" and by the fact that Native children were not allowed to attend public schools. Peratrovich began working for equal rights for Alaska's Native people. In 1945, Alaska passed the Anti-Discrimination Act, giving civil rights to Alaskan Natives. February 16, the day that the Act became law, is a state holiday known as Elizabeth Peratrovich Day.

Carl Ben Eielson: Aviation Pioneer

Carl Ben Eielson came to Fairbanks to teach high school science in 1922. Soon after, he became a pilot and delivered mail and supplies to remote villages. In 1928, Eielson and a copilot were the first to fly over the North Pole. Eielson's heroism won him many awards. In 1929, he died in a plane crash while trying to rescue passengers stranded on a ship along the Siberian coast.

Captain Michael Healy: Ship Captain

Michael Healy was born in Georgia in 1839 to a former African slave and a white plantation owner. Healy joined the U.S. Revenue Marine, (now the Coast Guard) and in 1883, became captain of the largest ship patrolling Alaskan waters. For twenty years, Healy's ship delivered supplies, protected the coast, and performed scientific research and rescues at sea. Today, the Coast Guard's largest Polar icebreaker research ship is named the Healy.

Cities and Villages

People living in Alaska's cities have a very different lifestyle than Alaskans living in towns, villages, or the remote bush. Yet all Alaskans live with the dramatic change of seasons and the incredible wilderness around them. For example, drivers in Fairbanks, Alaska's second largest city, have an unusual problem in winter—ice fog. Ice fog is a thick, white, blinding fog made of ice crystals and automobile exhaust. But residents have learned to cope with these sorts of conditions and continue on with their daily lives.

Anchorage, Alaska's largest city, includes Chugach State Park—a half-million-acre wilderness area. That is not to say there are no busy city sidewalks and crowds. "We have our malls, movie theaters, McDonalds, Taco Bells, just like anywhere

A summer solstice celebration is held on the banks of the Chena River in Fairbanks.

else in the states!" says Wasilla resident Georgia Beaudoin. "But in winter, I can take off out my driveway on my snow-machine and go anywhere!" Anchorage is a beautiful city with parks, museums, shopping malls, two universities, and office buildings.

Many Anchorage residents, who prefer wide-open spaces, have moved an hour's distance or more out of town. But rather than hop in their cars and head out on the highway, they fly into work. "Almost as many people who have drivers licenses have a plane," says Beaudoin, "People land their float planes on Lake Hood in downtown Anchorage, it's the busiest float plane terminal in the world!" More than half of Alaska's entire population lives in or near Anchorage, but the atmosphere still feels friendly and open. "People are different here," smiles Beaudoin. "We may have our problems and our crime, but you can stop and ask anyone for directions. No one is a stranger—we want to know our neighbors."

There are differences in rural and city lifestyles. Villages and cabins in the bush are sparsely settled far from cities and towns. People in remote Alaska rely on subsistence living for food for much of the year. Some villages do not have sewers or running water. Many schools are outdated and cannot afford enough teachers or new textbooks. Transportation is another problem for those living in remote areas. There are few roads so people travel by boat or snow-machine. Goods must be flown in, and that is expensive. There are also few doctors, dentists, nurses, or hospitals in these remote areas. As a result, people must depend on health aides who can only offer basic health care such as giving vaccines and treating minor cuts and bruises. If someone is very sick, he or she must be flown to a hospital some distance away.

"In extreme cases," says one North Slope resident, "like when there is a bad blizzard and planes can't land, we have medivac helicopters that come out." People living in villages count on each other to get by. "We look at family and community first," says a Yupik mother.

Outside traditional Tlingit villages, visitors are greeted by totem poles. These carvings of ravens, frogs, whales, eagles, and other creatures tell stories and legends, trace family ties, and mark special events. Though the phrase "low man on the totem pole" is meant to describe the least important person in a group, that is untrue of totem poles. The head carver usually carves the bottom figure himself, because he knows the lowest one is the easiest seen, so it must be perfect.

Festivals and the Outdoors

Alaskans by nature have a great sense of adventure and fun. Their celebrations are full of lively variety. Every May, Norwegian-Americans celebrate their heritage and the beginning of the fishing season. In Petersburg, the Little Norway Festival offers boat tours, traditional Norwegian costumes and dances, and the array of Scandinavian foods known as smorgasbord.

"Everyone goes to the state fair," says one Palmer native. "It's the most awesome fair anywhere. There is so much to do. and you see people, like maybe somebody you met once up in the North Pole, and there they are at the fair!" The Alaska State Fair in Palmer is a ten-day event loaded with entertainment, contests, and exhibits. If you are hungry, you will find foods to

Fireworks light up the sky above Anchorage during the annual Fur Rendezvous festivities.

fit any urge, from Mexican tacos, Greek gyros, Cajun gumbo, Texas barbeque, to fresh Bristol Bay salmon. Another long-running celebration is the winter Fur Rendezvous, which honors the early fur trappers. During this winter festival, people enjoy ice sculpture displays, sled-dog-pulling contests, an Eskimo blanket toss, snowshoe softball, and a dog-sled race.

Throughout southern Alaska, Native people host traditional celebrations called potlatches. Historically, potlatches honored the dead and were a religious ceremony that brought together spirits of the dead with the living. People sang, made speeches, prepared favorite foods of the ancestors, and gave away gifts. Potlatches remain an important event, in which people or events are honored with songs, dance, drumming, and foods, such as fry bread and roasted pig. Contests are held, such as tug of war, fish-cleaning, and net mending. You will also find other contests of strength and endurance at the Native Youth Olympics, held each year in Anchorage. More than one hundred teams of Native youths compete in contests that reflect traditional fishing and hunting skills, such as the stick pull, knee jump, and seal hop.

Nearly all of Alaska's festivals and events celebrate the outdoors. There are bird-watching festivals, such as the Copper River Shorebird Festival, the Sandhill Crane Festival in Fairbanks, and the Alaska Bald Eagle Festival in Haines. In Seward, a favorite winter event is the Polar Bear Jump-off, in which contestants dress in silly costumes and leap into the freezing ocean. Other activities include a parade, ice bowling, and an ugly fish toss. In March, Nome holds the Bering Sea Ice Golf Tournament, during which golfers actually play a round of golf on the frozen sea. Dog mushing is the official state sport, and throughout northern Alaska there are several major dog-sled races. The most famous is the Iditarod. During the Iditarod, fans line the trail route from Anchorage to Nome and cheer on their favorite teams.

Though many Alaskans spend long, cold, dark winters playing indoor sports like basketball, they would rather be

An ice sculpture of a dog-sled team is displayed during a winter fair.

outdoors. "You can't let the weather stop you," laughs a visitor to the Columbia glacier. Outdoor activities are boundless— people ski, hike, cycle, snow-machine, fish, hunt, kayak, sail, rock climb, backpack, and more. And in the summer, when the days are long, people get outdoors as much as they can. "Things are big here," says the woman by the glacier, "Alaska is like nowhere else!"

Calendar of Events

Iron Dog Race

In February, the snowmobilers compete in the world's longest snow-machine race. This 2,274-mile race stretches from Fairbanks to Nome to Wasilla. Most riders battle tricky winter weather conditions to finish in three days.

Anchorage Fur Rendezvous

This event—often called the Fur Rondy—has been held nearly every year for more than thirty years. The February festival started as an event that brought communities together and celebrated the important fur trade. Trappers and traders could show and sell their furs and products. Today the celebration includes a fireworks show, arts and crafts exhibits, a carnival, and competitions.

Iditarod Trail Sled-Dog Race

On the first Saturday in March, dog-sled mushers and their dog-sled teams line up in Anchorage to start the race to Nome. Most teams arrive in about nine days. Fans cheer along the route and at the finish line. During and after the race, people enjoy other events such as arts and crafts, music, dancing, and a reindeer potluck.

The Iditarod

Mayor's Midnight Sun Marathon

Racers gather on the first day of summer and race a traditional 26.2-mile marathon through Anchorage. On this day, racers and fans celebrate nearly twenty hours of Alaskan sunlight.

World Eskimo-Indian Olympics

In July, Native Alaskans and other people living in polar regions around the world come together in Fairbanks to compete in traditional survival skills. Among the events are the high-kick, ear pull, blanket toss, four-man carry, and other feats having to do with hunting and fishing.

Alaska State Fair

Every August, thousands travel by land, sea, and air to bring their vegetables, fruits, flowers, arts and crafts, and livestock to the fair in Palmer. There are delicious foods, games, fireworks, and concerts as well as entertaining contests such as: a parent-child look-alike contest, best scarecrow, a giant cabbage weigh-off, a pig-herding contest, and a joke and tall-tale festival.

Alaska Bald Eagle Festival

Birders and nature lovers from all over the world gather in November at the Alaska Chilkat Bald Eagle Preserve to watch the largest gathering of bald eagles in the world feast on an end-of-season run of wild salmon. Other events include photo workshops, art displays, and the release of rehabilitated eagles back into the wild.

Korean drummers perform at the state fair.

How It Works

Alaskans were pleased to become an official territory of the United States in 1912, but Alaskans felt the federal government in Washington, D.C., was too distant to properly govern them. In 1956, Alaskans held a constitutional congress and drafted a state constitution. Many politicians called it "one of the best, if not the best, state constitutions ever written." On January 3, 1959, Alaska was officially accepted into the Union.

Sitka was the first capital city of colonial Alaska, because it was where the Russian-America Company was based. But in 1880, shortly after the Americans took over, Juneau became the capital. Ringed by mountains and surrounded by the waters of the Inside Passage, Alaskans claim Juneau is one of the most beautiful capital cities in the world.

Alaskan Government

There are three levels of government in Alaska: borough, city, and state. Alaskan boroughs are like most other states' counties. They are made up of regions that include cities,

Alaska's capitol is one of the few state capitols that does not have a dome.

towns, and rural areas. There are sixteen boroughs in Alaska, governed by a group called an assembly. The head of the assembly is a mayor or a borough manager. The sixteen boroughs contain most of the state's population but only take up 44 percent of the state's land area. People living in the rest of the state all belong to a seventeenth borough called the

Branches of Government

The highest level of government in Alaska is the state government. It has three branches.

Executive The chief officer of the executive branch is the governor. He or she is elected to a four-year term. The governor appoints other important officials and suggests new laws. He or she also signs bills, which makes them law, or refuses to sign them, which is called a veto.

Legislative The legislative branch makes the laws and budgets the money needed to operate the government. There are two parts to the legislature: the House of Representatives and the Senate. There are forty representatives elected for two-year terms and twenty senators elected for four-year terms.

Judicial The judicial branch is a system of courts made up of a supreme court, a court of appeals, a superior court, and a district court. The supreme court supervises all other courts and rules on very important cases. If there is a disagreement with a lower court ruling, the court of appeals may decide the case. Superior courts are trial courts for most civil and criminal cases. District courts hear small civil cases and crimes such as traffic violations. These courts also issue search and arrest warrants.

"unorganized borough." They do not elect an assembly but instead are governed by the state legislature. City dwellers elect city councils that are led by a mayor or a city manager.

Native Claims

During the days of European and American settlement in Alaska, no treaties were ever signed with Native Alaskans. In 1924, the Indian Citizenship Act granted United States citizenship to Native Americans—including Alaska Natives—without taking away tribal rights and property. But by the time Alaska was made a state, Native Alaskans were worried that they were losing too much of their traditional lands. They formed a group called the Alaska Federation of Natives and asked the U.S. Congress for rights to their land. In 1971, Congress passed the Alaska Native Claims Settlement Act, which gave Alaskan Natives ownership of 44 million acres of land.

The act also formed thirteen Native regional corporations and two hundred village corporations. They were also granted nearly one billion dollars as a settlement for lands taken by Americans. Some of the duties of an Alaska Native corporation are to manage lands, provide education and cultural activities, and to handle resources such as fishing, mining, logging, and oil drilling. Some of the corporations are very wealthy, especially those that have oil on their land. All of them play a key role in local government.

How Alaska's Laws Are Made

In Alaska, citizens can propose or change a law by a process called initiative and referendum. In an initiative, citizens ask for a new law and write a petition. If enough people sign and agree to the initiative, it goes before all the voters in the next election. If people vote for the initiative, then it becomes law. To change a law, citizens can write a petition called a referendum. If enough citizens agree and sign the referendum, it is put before all the people for a vote. If the referendum wins, then the law is changed. For the most part, however, legislators in the House of Representatives and the Senate create or change most of the state's laws.

The draft of a law is called a bill. A representative or a senator must be responsible for a bill. But sometimes a citizen or a group of citizens ask their legislator to sponsor a bill. Once a bill is sponsored, it has to go through an official process before it can be approved and made into law. The bill that officially designated a state land mammal is an example of how this process worked.

In 1997, a first grade class at Kalifornsky Beach Elementary decided that Alaska should have a state land mammal. First, the students got their school involved, and then involved students and teachers across the whole state. They began by studying land mammals. The students voted for their favorites, based on how important the mammal was to the history and culture of the state. The moose won the most votes. The students agreed that the moose was their choice. They asked their senator to sponsor a bill to declare the moose the state land mammal. State Senator John Torgerson oversaw the writing and sponsoring of the bill. The bill was given a number, Senate Bill 265, and went to a committee for study. Committees are groups of lawmakers who are experts on certain subjects, such as agriculture, transportation, environment, health, education, or taxes. When a bill is being considered, citizens are encouraged to write letters to committee members or to call or visit them in person at their meetings. The students at Kalifornsky Elementary did just that. The committee members thought the bill was a good idea. The bill was presented to the entire senate. The senators passed the bill on February 22, 1998.

After a bill passes in one house, it must move on to the next. So the bill went to the House of Representatives. After going through the same process, the house passed the bill on April 17, 1998. Since both houses agreed that the moose would make a good state land mammal, the bill went to Governor Tony Knowles. The governor could do one of three things: he could sign the bill, which would make it law; he could veto the bill, which would mean that the bill would not become law; or he could do nothing, allowing the bill to become law after a short waiting period. Governor Knowles signed the state land mammal bill into law on May 1, 1998. This is an excellent example of how Alaskan residents can become involved with their government.

To find out which Alaskan legislators represent the different communities go to this Web site:
http://www.gov.state.ak.us/ltgov/elections/distcom.htm

5 Making a Living

Alaskan Farming

No one really thinks of farming when they think of Alaska, but more than a million acres of Alaska is farmland. Most of this farmland is in the Tanana and Matanuska valleys. There, and in a few other locations, farmers grow hay and vegetables. Many farms also raise dairy cattle, sheep, reindeer, and goats. On the Seward Peninsula, Native Alaskans raise reindeer for meat. Aleuts who live on the Aleutian chain raise reindeer and sheep.

Farming began in Alaska when the Great Depression hit the lower forty-eight states in the 1930s. Across the Mid-west and the Great Plains, farmers suffered from drought, grasshoppers, and low crop prices. President Franklin Roosevelt wanted to help the poorest of them so he gave land in Alaska's Matanuska Valley near Palmer to two hundred farmers, from Minnesota, Wisconsin, and Michigan. Winters there were bitterly cold and transportation costs were high, so few stayed on.

Snapdragons and large cabbage grow in the fertile soil of the Matanuska Valley.

Recipe for Alaska Wild Blueberry Cobbler

Several different types of edible berries grow well in Alaska. In summer, Alaskans enjoy picking these wild fruits and use them to make jams, desserts and other treats. Here is a recipe for tasty berry cobbler.

Ingredients:

4 cups fresh blueberries (you can use 4 cups of frozen unsweetened blueberries instead of fresh ones)

1 cup all-purpose flour

1/2 teaspoon baking powder

1 cup sugar

1 egg

1/4 cup butter

1/2 teaspoon margarine

Before preparing your cobbler, set the oven to 375 degrees. Be sure to have an adult help you.

Rub a 9 inch square baking pan with margarine, using a bit of paper towel. Wash the berries and pick off the stems. Spread the berries over the bottom of the greased pan.

In a small bowl, beat the egg with a fork and set aside. In a medium-sized bowl, stir the flour, baking powder, and sugar. Add the beaten egg to this flour mixture and stir the ingredients until crumbly.

Spread the mixture over the berries. Dot the top with small pats of butter. Bake at 375 degrees for 45 to 50 minutes. Ask an adult to help take the cobbler from the oven. Be sure to use oven mitts—the pan will be very hot! Cool the cobbler until it is warm, and serve with ice cream. Enjoy!

But the families of those that did, today live and work in one of the most beautiful valleys in the world.

The growing season is short—just June through September—but summer days are long. On some days, the sun never seems to set at all. With so much sun, Matanuska Valley farmers can grow truly giant vegetables. You can walk through fields and see a head of broccoli 7-feet wide, cabbages weighing 95 pounds, and stalks of Swiss chard 9 feet tall.

Sea Harvest

More Alaskans have jobs in the fishing industry than in any other state industry. Wild salmon are plentiful in Alaska. There are five types of salmon in Alaskan waters: King or Chinook—which is the largest and most valuable—sockeye, silver or coho, chum, and pink salmon. Other seafood harvested in Alaska are crab and shrimp. Halibut and bottom fish such as red snapper and ling cod are also popular catches.

Besides the fishermen, there are food processors that hurriedly clean, ice, and prepare the fish for the market. Other jobs in the fishing industry are shipbuilding and repair, gear and tackle, transportation, and marketing. For several decades, the fishing industry has had ups and downs. Today, fishermen complain that prices for fish are too low.

A deckhand on a salmon fishing boat hauls in a net full of fish.

Many say their problems stem from competition from fish farms that raise salmon in pens. These farms can supply markets year round and are not affected by weather conditions, seasonal changes, or the breeding schedule of the fish. But Alaska fishermen and seafood fans say nothing tastes as great as wild Alaska seafood. Some fishermen make a living selling their fish directly to customers by advertising on the Internet. "We spend more time selling than catching," says Joyce Adams, "but we love our salmon!"

Natural Riches

There are also plenty of natural resources to be found on land. Thick, green rainforests of cedar, hemlock, and spruce cover southeastern Alaska. Loggers have harvested timber in Alaska since it was a Russian colony. After railroads and shipping ports were built during World War II, logging companies were able to deliver millions of feet of lumber to markets around the world. Small coastal towns prospered from this increased business. However, today people disagree about the benefits of logging. Some want to continue to make a living from logging the forests and others want the government to protect the wilderness. All over southeastern Alaska, National Forest Service workers try to balance a healthy economy with a healthy environment.

Minerals provide Alaska with its most valuable industry. Minerals such as gold, silver, and zinc are mined in Alaska, but oil makes the most of the economy. Oil was first discovered in 1968 on the Alaska North Slope near Prudhoe Bay. Once Alaskans understood that the oilfield was twice the size of any other in North America, a building boom began. In 1977,

Oil production platforms in the Cook Inlet.

Alaskans finished the 800-mile pipeline over the permafrost from the Arctic Sea to the port of Valdez. During the project, thousands of workers came to Alaska, seeking high-paying construction jobs. Many decided to settle in the state. Once the oil began to flow, Alaska's treasury grew rich. Citizens voted to put some of the profits from oil sales into a special account called the Alaska Permanent Fund. Each year since, Alaska citizens receive a check for their share of earnings in the fund.

Over the years, the oil supply has declined, so Alaskans hope to find other ways for their economy to grow. Many want to drill for oil in the Arctic National Wildlife Refuge on the North Slope. Like most of the land in Alaska, the ANWR is owned by the federal government, so federal lawmakers must decide how the land is managed. Some want to drill for oil, and think that the refuge is a "flat, white nothingness."

At 6.5 miles per hour, a barrel's worth of oil takes five days to flow from Prudhoe Bay to Valdez through the Trans-Alaska Pipeline.

Others believe that the refuge is home to many wildlife species and one of the last unspoiled places on Earth.

Products & Resources

Reindeer

Reindeer

When the herds of wild caribou declined in the 1890s, missionaries imported reindeer from Siberia to Alaska to help feed Native Alaskans. Today, Native Alaskans herd reindeer on the Seward Peninsula and in other regions.

Western Hemlock

The Western hemlock is the most common tree growing in the rain forests of southeastern Alaska. More than 200 feet tall, this sturdy tree was once used to build mineshafts and railroad tracks. The hemlock today is harvested for building construction, plywood, and for making high quality paper.

Gold

Mining is the state's largest industry. Oil and gas are the most valuable products, but gold is the state mineral. Most of the gold mines are in the Interior. During the gold rush days, miners rinsed out gold by sloshing ore and gravel around in goldpans. Today, for sport or for profit, people can still pan for gold along stream banks or the beaches near Nome.

Alaska King Crab

Seafood lovers around the world also treasure the sweet-tasting, dark-red Alaska king crab. Each winter, Alaska crab fishermen brave the rough waters of the chilly Bering Sea, and work twenty hours a day to harvest their catch. Alaska king crabs can grow as large as 24 pounds and can measure 6 feet from leg to leg!

Fishing

The fishing industry provides many jobs for Alaskans across the state. Not only do Alaskans work on the commercial fishing boats that catch the seafood, but many also work in the plants and factories. These businesses are responsible for cleaning, preparing, packing, and sending tasty Alaskan seafood to customers around the world.

Tourism

Tourism is Alaska's third largest industry. More than one million tourists visit each year— usually in the summer months—to hike, fish, hunt, and enjoy the wildlife and scenery. They arrive by airplane, boat, or by driving the one highway that connects Alaska to the "Lower 48," the Alaska-Canada (Alcan) Highway that begins in Dawson Creek, British Columbia and crosses the border near Tok, Alaska.

Alaska Works

Not everyone in Alaska works as a fisherman, miner, or logger. There are many other types of work in government, military, and other service jobs. People in service jobs improve their communities by working as teachers, lawyers, bankers, restaurant workers, truck drivers, postal carriers, firefighters, police officers, pilots, tour guides, and more.

Many Alaskans are employed as educators or school administrators. This class in St. Paul is learning about the Aleut language.

The Arctic Region Supercomputing Center performs large and difficult research in science and engineering. The center is located at the University of Alaska in Fairbanks and was first built to serve the military. The supercomputers have names such as Yukon, Icehawk, and Iceberg and help scientists study ocean currents, tsunamis, the atmosphere, volcanoes, geology, genes, and arctic biology.

In the 1940s, the U.S. military saw that Alaska's geographic location could be important in the defense of North America. Before the outbreak of World War II, the government built docks, airfields, warehouses, bases, roads, railroads, and radar and communications installations. Today, more than 20,000 people are employed in the military at early warning radar sites in the Arctic or on bases near Anchorage and Fairbanks. There are two Army bases, Forts Wainwright and Richardson, and two Air Force bases, Eielson Air Force Base near Fairbanks and Elmendorf Air Force Base outside of Anchorage. Other government jobs are in local and state government, public schools, and public hospitals.

Tourism is one of Alaska's growing service industries. From the Gates of the Arctic National Park in the north, to the Misty Fjords National Monument in the southeast,

Safely situated on a viewing platform, tourists watch grizzly bears that live in Katmai National Park.

there is so much to see and do. Millions of tourists come to watch bears feed on salmon at Katmai Falls, to hear glaciers break up in Glacier Bay, or to see the Northern Lights in Barrow, as well as to kayak, hunt, fish, bird-watch, whale-watch, hike, and more. One tourist marvels, "We saw huge mountains, turquoise water, many water falls, humpback whales, Stellar sea lions, and glaciers—all up close and personal!"

For most Alaskans, the money from tourism is very welcome. However, many also feel that tourists can be too much of a good thing. Cruise ships are like giant floating cities, and often the crowds are too large for the small fishing villages they visit. Environmentalists are also upset about the wastewater the

Besides enjoying the state's breathtaking natural beauty, visitors to Alaska can also learn about the state's colorful history. In this photograph tourists are taking a carriage ride through historic parts of Skagway.

ships dump overboard. In other parts of the wilderness, hikers, kayakers, and sports fishermen say that tour buses and sight-seeing helicopters spoil the peaceful beauty everyone came to enjoy. But each year, more and more visitors come to admire Alaska's cities, villages, and parks. And so communities, business leaders, and government officials are working to make it easy for the Great Land to be enjoyed by all.

Transportation workers are key to Alaska's survival. The state is far from the rest of the world's markets. Little food is grown locally and few goods are manufactured, so citizens must ship in almost everything. There are only nine highways in the state. Though they are generally very scenic, some are quite rough. Truckers battle dusty, lonely, frozen roads to deliver food and necessities to remote towns and villages. Many towns and villages, including Juneau, have no roads leading to them at all. To reach Juneau and other southeast towns such as Ketchikan, Haines, and Skagway, travelers use either an airplane or the ferry system, called the Alaska Marine Highway.

Another means of transporting goods are the railroads. Many were first built to haul ore and timber and to serve the military. Now there is only one major railroad left in the state, the Alaska Railroad. It runs between Seward and Fairbanks. People who live near the railroad line and others who want to go out into the bush to hike and fish only need to wait along the side of the tracks and flag the train to stop. It is a very popular run, and one of the last "flagstop" railroads left in the world.

But the easiest means of getting to any city, village, or settlement is by air. Though costly, an airplane is often the only way for people to get the supplies and services they need.

Many citizens have a pilot's license and own an airplane. A bush pilot said that in the early years of flight he flew "into areas that weren't even on the map. Every flight back then was a grand adventure."

Alaskans, and visitors to Alaska, will likely agree that living or touring in the last frontier is still a very grand adventure.

One of the nation's most successful commercial airline companies is Alaska Airlines, begun in 1932 by a bush pilot in his three-seater floatplane.

Many Alaskans, like these two sport fishermen, commonly fly by float plane to reach their destination.

Alaska

The state flag was designed in 1926 by a Native Alaskan student named Benny Benson. The flag is blue with eight gold stars representing the constellation Ursa Major (known as the Big Dipper), along with the North Star. The blue represents both the color of the Alaskan sky as well as the color of the state flower, the forget-me-not. The stars represent Alaska's strength as well as its place as the northernmost state.

The state seal was originally designed in 1910 while Alaska was still a territory. The circular seal is gold, and shows the Northern Lights glowing over tall mountains. There are a smelter to represent mining and a train and ships that represent transportation. Other resources are honored with pictures of trees, fish, and a farmer, his horse, and some wheat. The seal represents Alaska's great wealth.

State Flag and Seal

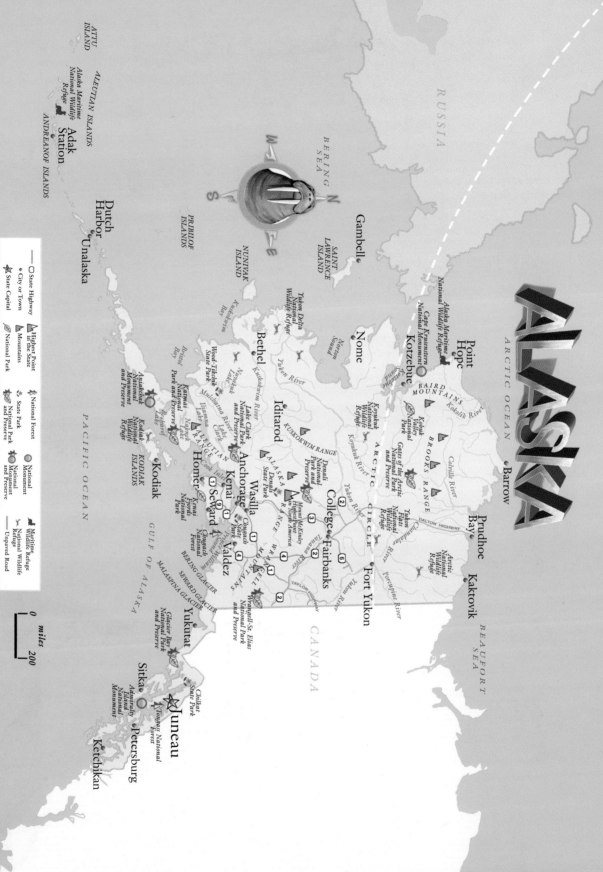

ALASKA

ARCTIC OCEAN

RUSSIA

BERING SEA

BEAUFORT SEA

PACIFIC OCEAN

GULF OF ALASKA

CANADA

Barrow

Kaktovik
Prudhoe Bay

Point Hope
Kotzebue

Fort Yukon

College
Fairbanks
Valdez

Anchorage
Wasilla
Kenai
Seward
Homer

Kodiak

Bethel

Nome

Gambell

Idiarod

Yakutat

Sitka
Petersburg

Juneau

Ketchikan

Dutch Harbor
Unalaska

Adak Station

ATTU ISLAND

Alaska Maritime National Wildlife Refuge

ALEUTIAN ISLANDS

ANDREANOF ISLANDS

PRIBILOF ISLANDS

NUNIVAK ISLAND

SAINT LAWRENCE ISLAND

KODIAK ISLANDS

ALEUTIAN RANGE

ALASKA RANGE

BROOKS RANGE

BAIRD MOUNTAINS

WRANGELL MOUNTAINS

KUSKOKWIM RANGE

Yukon River

Colville River

Kobuk River

Koyukuk River

Porcupine River

Tanana River

Kuskokwim River

ARCTIC CIRCLE

Norton Sound

Kotzebue Sound

Kvichak Bay

Bristol Bay

Kuskokwim Bay

Cook Inlet

MALASPINA GLACIER
SEWARD GLACIER
BERING GLACIER

DALTON HIGHWAY
TAYLOR HIGHWAY

Cape Krusenstern National Monument

Alaska Maritime National Wildlife Refuge

Kobuk Valley National Park

Gates of the Arctic National Park and Preserve

Arctic National Wildlife Refuge

Yukon Flats National Wildlife Refuge

Koyukuk National Wildlife Refuge

Denali National Park and Preserve

Denali State Park

Mount McKinley
Highest Point in North America

Chugach State Park

Wrangell-St. Elias National Park and Preserve

Chugach National Forest

Kenai Fjords National Park

Katmai National Park and Preserve

Lake Clark National Park and Preserve

Aniakchak National Monument and Preserve

Kodiak National Wildlife Refuge

Wood-Tikchik State Park

Yukon Delta National Wildlife Refuge

Togiak National Wildlife Refuge

Glacier Bay National Park and Preserve

Chilkat State Park

Admiralty Island National Monument

Tongass National Forest

Iliamna Lake

Becharof Lake

Naknek Lake

Cohalik River

Legend

- State Highway
- City or Town
- State Capital
- National Park
- Highest Point in the State
- Mountains
- State Park
- National Forest
- National Monument
- National Park and Preserve
- National Monument and Preserve
- Maritime Wildlife Refuge
- National Wildlife Refuge
- Unpaved Road

0 miles 200

Alaska's Flag

Words by Marie Drake
Music by Elinor Dusenbury

State Song

More About Alaska

Books

Bial, Raymond. *The Tlingit*. New York: Benchmark Books, 2003.

Brown, Tricia, ed. *Children of the Midnight Sun: Young Native Voices of Alaska*. Anchorage: Alaska Northwest Books, 1998.

Corral, Kimberly and Hannah Corral. *My Denali: Exploring Alaska's Favorite National Park*. Seattle, WA: Alaska Northwest Books, 1995.

Hiscock, Bruce. *The Big Caribou Herd: Life in the Arctic National Wildlife Refuge*. Honesdale, PA: Boyds Mills Press, 2003.

Riddles, Libby. *Storm Run: the Story of the First Woman to Win the Iditarod Sled Dog Race*. Seattle, WA: Sasquatch Books, 2002.

Sherrow, Victoria. *The Exxon Valdez:Tragic Oil Spill*. Springfield, NJ: Enslow, 1998.

Web sites

Official Alaska Government Site for Kids:

www.state.ak.us/kids

U.S. National Parks and State Parks in Alaska:

http://www.us-national-parks.net/state/ak.htm

About the Author

Ruth Bjorklund lives on Bainbridge Island, a ferry ride away from Seattle, Washington, and two ferry rides away from Skagway, Alaska. She, her husband, and their two children plan to paddle their kayaks in Glacier Bay someday very soon.

Index

Page numbers in **boldface** are illustrations.